from the Cradle to the Grave

Elizabeth Eisenberg

© 1992

ISBN 0 946404 87 9

Printed and Published by
J. H. Hall & Sons Limited, Siddals Road, Derby
Printers and Stationers since 1831
Telephone: Derby (0332) 45218
Facsimile: (0332) 296146

 THE DERBYSHIRE HERITAGE SERIES

'. . . birth and death were considered inevitable, illness and accidents inescapable, and all were treated with a mixture of religion, superstition and, sometimes, witchcraft.'

Birth, Babies and Baptism

PREGNANCY

According to a woman's circumstances, the confirmation that she has conceived can send her into transports of delight or cast her into the depths of despair. And so it has been from time immemorial.

In bygone days when the mortality rate for babies and young children was alarmingly high, there was an urgent need to perpetuate the family and births were welcomed both in and out of wedlock. So important was it in Medieval times to 'fill the cradles' that the Derbyshire custom of 'going to the woods' on the eve of May Day, condemned by the Puritans as a 'shameful frolic,' was actually encouraged by many parents. Boys and girls, setting out ostensibly to gather flowering branches for decorating their homes, often did not return until dawn and it was said that 'scarcely one third returned home undefiled.' Consequently, a substantial increase in the number of births took place in the following January.

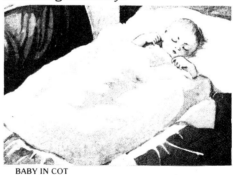
BABY IN COT

Conscious of the declaration in the marriage service that Holy Matrimony was 'ordained for the procreation of children,' every newly married couple looked forward eagerly to the birth of their first child. If, a year after the wedding, there was no sign that the wife was breeding, they could expect to endure taunts and derisory jokes and receive much facetious advice on methods of ensuring conception.

Derbyshire people put their faith in a diet of frumenty (wheat boiled in milk with added spices) and strong cheese for the husband with an infusion of mistletoe berries added to his first drink in the morning. Nuts and figs were also recommended, the latter because of their many seeds, and tansy juice taken morning and night since tansy grows where rabbits, prolific breeders, abound.

A shovelful of manure placed beneath the conjugal bed was one of the oldest Derbyshire methods of dealing with the problem and, as a last resort, the couple were advised that the act of copulation should take place, weather permitting, out in the fields with the wife lying over a mole hill, this position causing the curve of her body to facilitate conception. Sneezing at the time of orgasm was thought to prevent ovulation.

A reason for barrenness was often attributed to the prospective parents having the same coloured complexion. One dark and one fair would be more likely to procreate.

A variety of means was resorted to in determining whether or not a woman was in the family way. The most common of these in north Derbyshire was for her to urinate on a steel knitting needle which would turn green if she was pregnant. A distinctive smell in a woman's breath was said to be recognised by experienced old women at the beginning of pregnancy.

In order to prevent a miscarriage, pounded rose petals mixed with honey and eaten three times a day were recommended and honey, taken in quantities was believed to help in producing a sweet tempered offspring.

A mother-to-be was invariably warned against making sudden movements of her body. Pulling a cork out of a bottle was thought to be dangerous and stretching upwards could cause the baby to be strangled by the umbilical cord. Consequently, clothes lines were lowered to the height of a woman's armpits. A pregnant woman was advised to avoid looking at a dead body and sustaining a shock or a fright was thought to cause birthmarks on the baby. These were also attributed to particular foods like strawberries or pickled onions. Excessive heartburn meant that the child would be born with a lot of hair.

Culpeper, the 17th century physician, maintained that the attitude of a woman's mind during pregnancy had a bearing on the nature of the unborn child and warned expectant mothers against giving way to ill-temper, fear or grief. On the other hand, he believed that their changing moods and fancies should be tolerated.

'Er munna be thwarted,' was an expression used in Derbyshire. Centuries ahead of his time, Culpeper made the astonishing suggestion that a bath once a week would be beneficial. He also recommended exercise for he believed that poor people who worked hard produced more and stronger children.

BOY OR GIRL

There is always much speculation concerning the sex of the baby. The preference in agricultural districts of the county used to be for a 'turnip picker' rather than a 'pot washer' although many mothers hoped for a girl first who would grow up to be useful in looking after subsequent children.

Because of the ancient belief that birth and death were controlled by the moon, many people were convinced that a male child was conceived when the moon was rising, a female when it was on the wane.

Experiments to discover the child's sex varied in different parts of Derbyshire. In the Peak district a woman would hold her wedding ring, suspended from a thread, over her stomach. If the baby was a boy, the ring would swing to and fro, or round and round if it was a girl.

In the southern part of the county around Derby there was a theory that domestic fowls could distinguish the difference in sex of unborn children for it was said that, when a woman fed the fowls while carrying a boy child 'in utero,' the hens would clamour round her and the cockerel would walk away.

There has always been a belief that different ways of 'carrying' can indicate the child's sex. 'All at the front for a girl, all at the back for a boy' is quoted to this day in spite of the fact that the opposite frequently proves this supposition unreliable.

At one time it was considered unwise to tempt Providence by taking delivery of a cot or pram before the baby was born in case it did not survive. This point of view has been superseded in Derbyshire by the belief that, if the cot or pram is not paid for outright, the child will grow up too poor to pay for its own coffin.

UNWANTED BABIES

For an unmarried girl, brought up in a strictly religious family, to become pregnant was a disaster. Working girls were constantly threatened by their parents, 'Bring trouble home and it's the workhouse for you.' Indeed, it is not unknown in early Victorian times for an employee of one of Derbyshire's industrialists to be given the sack on account of his daughter's 'misbehaviour.'

Eventually, however, after tears and recriminations, and if a wedding could not be arranged, the little 'love child' would usually be accepted and brought up with the younger end of the girl's family while the mother returned to domestic service and sent home a portion of her wages for the child's upbringing.

Upper class young ladies in the same situation were customarily dispatched for 'a little holiday,' sometimes abroad. The baby would be adopted by a suitable family or else brought up by a competent nurse and finally restored to its mother in the guise of a distant relation who had been orphaned.

It was, possibly, the middle class parents who suffered most when a daughter brought shame on them in such a way. If a face-saving marriage was out of the question, it was not unknown for the girl to be driven to suicide or else to attempt to conceal the birth, sometimes with tragic results.

In Scarcliffe church is a beautiful alabaster monument, reputed to be 800 years old, of the Lady Constantia de Frecheville and her baby daughter, its tiny hand reaching out to the mother's face. Unmarried and pregnant and abandoned by the child's father, she was left to face the disgrace alone.

Soon after the child was born she ran away with it into the Scarcliffe woods where she wandered aimlessly until she heard the church curfew bell and the sound guided her home. In gratitude, she left in her will five acres of land to pay for the regular ringing of this bell each night for ever. Now it can be

LADY CONSTANTIA DE FRECHEVILLE

photo - Derbyshire Life

heard during the three weeks before Christmas and the three weeks after when Lady Constantia is said to haunt the woods with her child.

For a married woman with a large family and a husband on a starvation wage, if not unemployed, another child was an unwelcome burden and many mothers prayed that it would be born 'a little angel.' Until early this century, contraceptives were almost unknown and, anyway difficult to obtain and too expensive for the poor to afford them. Syringing after intercourse was recommended but could be difficult if the bedroom was shared by a number of children and the only supply of water was from a pump in the back yard.

Condoms made of leather or little sponges soaked in a sperm-killing liquid and introduced into the vagina seemed to be the only alternatives to 'coitus interruptus' — (book to Sheffield but alight at Dronfield, as Chesterfield people phrased it).

As soon as a woman suspected she was 'caught,' she resorted to the time-worn 'treatments' like taking strong laxatives, jumping off the garden wall or creeping, head first, downstairs. Finding these of no avail, she would turn to the use of penny-royal, then to consuming hot gin in large quantities together with indiscriminate doses of quinine, available at most chemists as a 'regulariser.'

Finally, if the use of an 'instrument' did not bring about the desired result, it was usually possible to discover some woman, known as 'Auntie,' who would 'see you all right, love' for a consideration.

Procuring an abortion was a criminal offence. In the 1930's a girl went to an address she had been given in Ripley. This information was always supplied by word of mouth and never written down. The door opened to her knock and she inquired if 'Auntie' was in.

'Auntie's gone down the line for three years', shouted the man in reply to her query. 'And for helping the likes of you,' he added, slamming the door in her face.

For generations, there was a widespread conviction that an abortion, if brought about before the child quickened, was justifiable. A questionnaire put to 3,000 women in this country in 1936 revealed that 35% of them had induced an abortion by means of 'interference.' With the introduction of the oral contraceptive, the Pill, in the 1960's, the birth rate began to fall steadily but a survey in 1966 produced figures showing that in that year in Britain about 85,000 women had attempted to procure a miscarriage. It is tempting to speculate on the number who did not admit to having done so.

In January, 1939 the Derby Evening Telegraph reported the case of a Derby woman, aged 36, who had died as the result of an illegal abortion. Throughout the seventeen years of her married life, said the coroner, she had been either pregnant or recovering from childbirth. He spoke understandingly of the desperate feeling she must have experienced on finding herself pregnant yet again and he remarked that many women would identify with her.

'The practice', he added, 'is rife in this town and these abortionists, for a few pieces of silver, risk a woman's life.'

INFANTICIDE

Derby Assize Court was, at one time, noted for its leniency when dealing with the murder of a newly born child, obviously taking into consideration the state of the mother's mind at the time. Women convicted of this crime were rarely condemned to death.

The first woman in Derby to be sentenced to death for more than twenty years was Mary Dilkes who, in 1754 was found guilty of leaving her bastard child on a sandbank on the Holmes, an island in the River Derwent. She was executed in the presence of a large crowd of spectators.

In February 1796, a man of seventy, James Preston, was jointly sentenced to death with Susannah Moreton for the murder of her baby. He was executed but she gained a last

DERBY ASSIZE COURT

photo — Frank Rodgers

minute reprieve on the morning fixed for her execution.

Hannah Halley was convicted at Derby Assizes in March 1822 for causing her child's death by placing it in scolding hot water. Employed at Darley Abbey Mills, she said the devil had impelled her to commit the crime.

Out of the nineteen cases of wilful murder of a newborn child brought before the Derby Assize Court between the years 1837 and 1860, only one mother was found guilty. The others were convicted of concealment of birth which was punishable by a prison sentence ranging from three months to two years.

In 1844 Hannah Slack was aquitted of being responsible for her baby's death in spite of a doctor having certified that the child had died through taking arsenic.

A child newly born to Elizabeth Vicars in 1850 was discovered with a tape tied tightly round its neck but the mother was found guilty only of concealment of birth and sentenced to one year's imprisonment.

After giving birth to an illegitimate baby in 1880, Mary Wright was turned out of the house by her father. As a result, Mary drowned the child in a pond on Bonsall Moor. She was found guilty of murder but her sentence was commuted to life imprisonment.

GIVING BIRTH

An astonishing number of women interviewed early this century said they had no idea how a baby was born until they were, themselves, confined. To discuss any aspect of sex, or for that matter any bodily function, was considered indelicate and was avoided at all costs even between mothers and married daughters or husbands and wives.

The process of giving birth, described in the Book of Common Prayer as a time of 'great pain and peril,' has varied through the centuries from a private ordeal by the mother alone, to a social occasion attended by crowds of female friends and relatives.

Unmarried females, whatever their ages, were traditionally excluded from the spectacle and so were children who, in

Derbyshire, were told that baby girls grew in the parsley bed and baby boys in the nettle bed, a variation on the gooseberry bush legend.

Until the first World War, most confinements took place at home, supervised by the local midwife. Often untrained but experienced in delivering babies, she was also efficient in laying out a dead body.

To ensure an easy labour it was thought advisable for the woman to lie in the direction of the current in the nearest river or stream.

'Same road as t'Darren flows,' they said in Derbyshire, the Darren being an old name for the Derwent. In the west of the county, 'Lay her t'Wye way,' was often heard.

It was also considered expedient to unlock all the doors in the house and to untie or loosen every knot.

Raspberry leaf tea was administered in quantities to reduce the pain and, in north Derbyshire, it was customary for a friend or relative to provide a Groaning Cake. This contained, among other ingredients, hempseed, rhubarb juice and dandelion roots mixed with a generous allowance of gin. The patient was given one or two slices to hasten the birth while the rest was divided among the other females in the house. Any childless woman would be given a piece, on request, in the belief that it would help her to conceive.

The yolk of an egg, beaten with saffron and sugar and followed by a drink of ale was another remedy thought to speed the delivery.

In the 17th century an eagle stone, found in the old ironstone grounds of north-east Derbyshire and believed to have magnetic properties on account of the vein of metal it contained, was kept at hand for a woman in labour to grasp in order to draw out the baby more quickly from the womb. This stone was often fastened round her thigh.

If the patient was making little progress and her condition gave cause for anxiety, a doctor would be sent for. In country districts this often necessitated a walk of three or four miles by the husband to the doctor's house. Add to this the time it took for the doctor to dress, harness his horse and make his way to the home of the patient and the worst could have happened before he arrived. This often occurred for, because of the difficulty in finding the money for his fee, a doctor was called only as a last resort.

Home births for both mothers and babies showed a lower mortality rate than those taking place in institutions. In workhouses or infirmaries a patient in labour was frequently left to the attention of other inmates, many of them old, ignorant or even mentally defective.

When required to attend a confinement in an institution a doctor usually refused to waste his time on a slow labour and used instruments to expedite the birth. Some medical men took the same course in a prolonged home confinement, especially if the patient belonged to the poorer working class.

From the 17th century onwards there was an increase in puerperal fever which accounted for the deaths of many mothers, particularly those in a charitable establishment like the Poor Law Infirmary in Chesterfield where, it was said, women lying-in after a delivery were mixed with inmates suffering from infectious diseases.

Doctors, at one time, considered the study of midwifery 'an occupation degrading to gentlemen' and, until the late 18th century, it was thought improper for any man to be in the vicinity when a woman was giving birth. It was said that many expectant mothers made their husbands promise not to send for a doctor on any account. They were convinced that the suffering of a difficult labour was preferable to having a man in attendance.

Such was the modesty of women in early Victorian times that when a doctor was present at a confinement he was supplied with a sheet, one end of which was tied round his neck as he stood at the foot of the bed, the other end being fastened under the armpits of the patient. In this way he was able to examine the patient 'by feel' and complete the delivery without seeing her nakedness. This saved both his and the expectant mother's embarrassment.

Medical students were trained, when making any examination on a woman, to keep their eyes on the ceiling.

ANAESTHETICS
Midwives were known to disapprove of the custom of giving

frequent drinks of gin to a woman in labour as this reduced her energy for pulling on the roller towel attached to the bottom bed rail during each contraction while the lookers-on shouted encouragement. But draughts of henbane, infusions of poppies or briony roots were popular aids for alleviating the severity of the pains.

However, it was widely believed that to seek relief from the agony by any means was contrary to the wishes of the Almighty. Called 'The Curse of Eve,' the suffering in childbirth was said to be God's punishment for Eve's sins. 'In sorrow shalt thou bring forth children,' was quoted from the scriptures and, in 1847, the growing practice of using anaesthetics in childbirth aroused much criticism and was vigorously condemned, predictably by men and, in particular, by the clergy.

QUEEN VICTORIA

Only after Queen Victoria agreed to be given chloroform for the birth of her 8th child did the practice, thereafter known as 'Chloroform à la Reine,' become acceptable and the opposition finally died down.

More than one mother in Derbyshire named her new daughter 'Anaesthesia' because of her astonishment and delight on coming round to find that the baby had been born.

A custom, faithfully followed in Derbyshire, was to carry the afterbirth three times round the beehives so that the bees would protect the child from misfortune. It was then placed on a fire to burn and the number of times it 'popped' was thought to indicate the number of future babies to be born to the mother.

In the event of a haemorrhage, the mother was given a potion made from boiled Shepherd's Purse, a flowering weed, and pancakes used as poultices were applied to her stomach

13

but the failure to stop persistent bleeding was the cause of many maternal deaths.

PREDICTIONS

The day of the week on which a child was born was believed to shape its destiny.

> *'Monday's child is fair of face,*
> *Tuesday's child is full of grace,*
> *Wednesday's child is full of woe,*
> *Thursday's child has far to go,*
> *Friday's child is loving and giving,*
> *Saturday's child must work for a living.*
> *But the child that is born on the Sabbath day*
> *Is bonny and blythe and good and gay.'*

This rhyme has been quoted for centuries everywhere in England but in Derbyshire the following was once popular.

> *'Born on Sunday it's the child of God,*
> *Born on Monday will smart 'neath the rod,*
> *A Tuesday born child has beauty and grace,*
> *A Wednesday's child seldom stays in one place,*
> *A Thursday's child is thrifty and clean,*
> *A Friday's child is not fit to be seen*
> *And a Saturday's child will be poor and mean.'*

Babies born earlier in the day were thought to have a better chance of survival, — 'the later the hour, the shorter the life' — and a child born during the waxing of the moon could be expected to thrive whereas those born while the moon was on the wane would have a constant struggle against adversity.

Maytime was considered unlucky for the birth of infants and young animals alike, all born in that month being difficult to rear. It was a fortunate child whose birthday fell during the twelve days of Christmas for this prevented it from suffering any accident or sudden death. The exception was December 28th, Childermas Day, the anniversary of the date when King Herod ordered the massacre of every male Hebrew child. Boys born on this day could expect persecution all their lives.

A baby born 'feet first,' known as a 'footling,' could grow up to have the power of healing and a caul (part of the membrane) covering its head at birth was an indication that it would not die from drowning. It was believed that a sailor who took a caul to sea with him need never fear shipwreck and any female in possession of one would have a safe delivery when confined.

Holding out its right hand soon after birth showed that the child would accumulate riches. Raising its hand above its head foretold that it would become a 'gaffer.'

It was the custom for visitors to place in the baby's hand a silver sixpence or a threepenny bit and to note the reaction. If the child grasped the coin tightly, it was a sign that it would acquire great wealth; if he failed to hold it, debts would play a significant part in its future life.

> 'A dimple in its chin, a living coming in,
> A dimple in its cheek, a living to seek'

was often quoted but to be born with a tooth meant that the child would be greedy.

A seventh child was expected to display supernatural powers when it reached maturity and be able to foretell the future.

TRADITIONS AND PRACTICES

In some parts of North Derbyshire there was a superstition that a baby weighed at birth would not thrive and, in the south of the county, mothers were persuaded that it was harmful to bath a child in the first few days of its life and washing its head during that time was particularly dangerous.

A common belief was held throughout the county that the first bath should be given in water to which wine had been added as this would increase the baby's strength. Traditionally, it was important to wash the child's right hand first to prevent it developing 'light fingers,' that is a propensity to steal.

Before the baby's first feed it was given a drink of Cinder Tea. This was boiled water into which a red hot coke had been dropped. Thought to clear the child's bowels, it was also looked upon as a means of keeping the devil away.

An old custom, prevalent everywhere in Derbyshire, was to lay the new born child's head on an open book in order to ensure that it would make a good scholar.

'Dinna bother wi' that,' said a young Ashover farmer. 'We want none o' them sort. Better put his head on a shovel.'

The practice of binding a child's limbs to keep them straight was continued well into the 19th century and my mother remembered seeing, in her childhood, young babies with veils over their faces. At that time there was a belief that it was harmful for a child's eyes to be exposed to the light until it was a few months old.

STILLBIRTHS

Stillborn babies were often buried in the same grave as a man, woman or child who had died about the same time. Relatives of these people welcomed the dead child in the belief that it acted as a passport to Heaven for the other corpse.

Otherwise, a stillborn baby or one who had died before being baptised was buried in unconsecrated ground situated on the north side of the church. Called the 'Devil's Side,' this plot was also used for the interment of suicides and criminals.

To tread on the grave of a stillborn child was thought to promote the risk of developing 'Churchyard Itch' or 'Grave Scab' which caused sufferers to have a burning skin. This complaint was said to be relieved only by constant prayer.

In 1538 parish priests were ordered to keep registers of baptisms but no records were made of stillbirths nor of children who died before they were christened. The registration of live births was introduced in 1837 though not obligatory until 1874 but records of stillbirths and unbaptised babies were not made compulsory until late in the last century.

A speedy rise in the birthrate took place in the second half of the 18th and continued throughout the 19th century but a shocking number of babies died within a few weeks of their birth. Friends and neighbours calling to look at a new baby would, more often than not, shake their heads and say, 'Doesn't look as if it's come to stay.'

Some were born puny and underweight on account of the mother's health, permanently undermined by endless pregnancies, insanitary living conditions and an inadequate diet for mothers have always supplied their husbands and children with more and better food than they have themselves.

LYING — IN

As always, the length of the lying-in period depended on the mother's health and circumstances. Better off women who could afford help with the housework and care of their other children took things easily and made little exertion for a month at least. Working class mothers often left their beds and coped with housework and children the day after they were confined.

'After the delivery,' directed Culpeper in his 'Book of Birth' published more than three hundred years ago, 'the mother should be given strong food and wine, avoiding salt meats, garlic and intoxicating liquor.'

In Derbyshire, however, the popular diet for a nursing mother was Caudle. This consisted of thin oatmeal gruel, spiced and mixed with rum, which was said to increase the milk supply. In north Derbyshire, the same ingredients with added flour were made into a Hasty Pudding to be eaten with honey or syrup.

Suckling a baby has always been regarded as a form of contraception, albeit an unreliable one, and for that reason some mothers continued to breast feed their children for two or three years. When my mother was still feeding me at the age of thirteen months, she asked a neighbour, the mother of a large family, if she thought this was a mistake.

'Bless you, no,' was the reply. 'Our Gregory (her youngest) used to pull me down for it the minute he got home from school. He never ailed anything and he's the strongest lad they've ever had working at Moor Farm.'

It is recorded that Queen Elizabeth the First was not weaned until she was twenty-five months old.

In contrast was the mother who was anxious to become

17

pregnant again and consequently employed a 'wet nurse' to suckle her child. There was no shortage of such women available on account of the enormous number of babies who died at birth or soon afterwards.

A wet nurse was chosen for her moral character rather than for the quantity and quality of her milk for it was believed that human vices passed to the child through the milk on which they were reared.

Culpeper recommended that a wet nurse should be fed well and should 'abstain from copulation and passions' which might disturb her supply of milk.

The alternative to a wet nurse was to feed the baby on either cow's or goat's milk by means of a cow horn. This practice was not popular on account of the fear that the child might come to resemble the animal which was the source of its sustenance.

In the 18th century it became unpopular for mothers to breast-feed their own babies so wet nurses were much in demand and were well paid by the aristocracy. 'Nursing' their own children grew more acceptable in the 19th century but, in the 1920's when flat, boyish figures were fashionable, women again turned against it and resorted to artificial feeding, bottles having by this time supplanted the cow horns.

On getting up and leaving the bedroom for the first time, it was important for the mother, holding the baby, to 'go up before going down.' This was to ensure that the child would rise in the world and, if there were no attic stairs to climb, the mother would step on a chair before going downstairs. Once in the kitchen, she would poke the fire thus establishing that she had become a part of the household once more.

CHURCHING

After a woman had been confined she was not supposed to leave her own premises until she had been churched for, until this ceremony had taken place, she was considered unclean and likely to spread bad luck wherever she went.

By crossing a stream she could contaminate the water, by coming into contact with a pregnant woman, she could harm the unborn child and by entering someone's house she could bring misfortune on all the inhabitants.

The 'Churching of Women' service took place as soon as possible after the birth and was looked upon as a purification ritual. The mother was directed to 'come to church decently apparelled' and give thanks to God for her safe deliverance from the 'great danger of childbirth.'

At one time it was customary for the woman being churched to hold a candle while the priest recited the prayers of thanksgiving and, if convenient, she could receive communion before making the 'accustomed offering' of money, a substitute for the ancient burnt offering.

ASHOVER CHURCH   photo — Frank Rodgers

'When ye woman comes to be churched,' states an ancient rule of All Saints' Church, Ashover, 'she giveth six pence to ye Minister and one penny to ye clerk.'

BAPTISM

Until earlier this century it was considered expedient for a child to be baptised as soon as possible after it was born. One reason for this haste was the ancient belief that, until an infant was christened, it was at the mercy of witches and evil spirits attempting to take possession of its soul.

Various methods of protecting the child from this hazard were employed. In Derbyshire it was the custom to cover the baby, if it was a boy, with an article of dress belonging to its mother or, for a baby girl, with a garment of her father's. Afraid that demons might steal their baby and leave a 'changeling,' mothers used to pin the child's clothes to a pillow.

There was a widespread belief that if a child died before having been christened, it would not be admitted to the Kingdom of Heaven and its soul would be condemned to remain on earth in the form of a butterfly or a moth. Consequently, if a newborn baby appeared to be sickly, a clergyman was hurriedly sent for with a request for a private baptism. This he had permission to carry out on finding 'great cause and necessity.'

Baptism was believed to improve a child's health and, until quite recently, the mother of a baby which was not thriving would be advised, often by non-religious people, to have it christened without delay.

'They come on better after a splash o' font watter,' was a local saying.

'Lay Baptism' has always been permitted in cases of emergency when no clergyman was available. Bess of Hardwick's husband, the Earl of Shrewsbury, christened their baby grandson because Queen Elizabeth refused to allow a priest to officiate while Mary, Queen of Scots, was in residence as a prisoner with them.

Before the Reformation in England it was customary for infants to be totally immersed when baptised, hence the size and depth of old fonts. 'Water straight from Heaven' was considered desirable for the purpose and, even after tap water was installed, it was the custom to collect rain water for use in the font.

In 1602, a rector at Sudbury was criticised because he 'kepte fishe in ye fonte' and christened babies with the same water.

At the point in the service when the child was given a name, the priest, being first assured that the infant was healthy enough to undergo the shock of immersion, would 'dip it in the water discreetly and warily.'

To prevent bad luck, the baby's name was never used until after the christening and was often kept a secret from anyone outside the family.

'How is little Jeremy?' called a neighbour over the garden wall and the mother was so horrified that a different name was immediately chosen and not revealed until the church ceremony took place.

The elder of twins was always baptised first but, in the case of one of each sex, the boy was named before the girl, otherwise it was thought that he would grow up effeminate.

After the service, water from the font was taken home, with the clergyman's permission, and was used in cases of illness, especially for sponging a child's body to reduce a fever or for rinsing out a baby's mouth to relieve teething troubles. It was also thought to be a cure for skin complaints. In some churches it was found necessary to fit the covers of fonts with locks to prevent the water being stolen.

In the 18th century public baptisms took place in rivers or wells, the first one recorded in Derby being the River Derwent near the Morledge in 1791. It was said that the water of St. Alkmund's well was noted for its healing properties and 'many screaming babies were dipped therein.'

Fonts were made shallower when christenings began to be carried out by pouring water only over the infant's head and face. This was never wiped away in case some misfortune might follow and it was the custom for a godparent to spit on the baby's face for luck.

The more lustily the child cried during the ceremony, the more successful its future life would be, according to an old superstition. An infant that endured the ritual without making a sound was thought to be 'too good to live' and not likely to live very long. It was therefore prodded and pinched in order to make it scream in the belief that its 'baptismal cries' would drive all 'evil dispositions' from its body.

On leaving the church it was customary to take the baby to the Manor House where it was presented to the Lord or Lady of the Manor who placed in its hand a silver coin, traditionally a sixpence or a threepenny bit. These were often treasured during the whole of the child's life and passed on as family heirlooms.

The Book of Common Prayer dictates that clergymen should 'admonish the people that they defer not the baptism of their children longer than the first or second Sunday after the birth.' This is so that no time may be lost before the godparents renounce, on the child's behalf, 'the World, the Flesh and the Devil.'

At one time, however, the belief that baptism could eradicate all mortal sins caused many people to postpone it as late in life as possible so that their accumulated misdemeanours might be forgiven 'en bloc.' The exception to this practice occurred in times of war or pestilence when the expectation of life was reduced and the need for baptism became urgent.

During the time of the Plague in Derbyshire, for instance, babies were taken to church to be christened soon after they were born, their mothers still being confined.

Courtship, Weddings and Marriage

COURTSHIP

Courtship was once defined as 'a lively, entertaining prologue to a dull, uninteresting play.'

In primitive times men obtained their mates by pursuit and capture followed by a blow on the head. Women, traditionally, made the chase difficult but they were usually willing captives.

Today's course of action is more subtle but may still be described as 'a man pursuing a woman until SHE captures HIM.'

'Better marry ower the midden (dung heap) than ower the moors,' was a Derbyshire saying, meaning it is safer to choose a wife or a husband nearer home than from unfamiliar territory.

Courting a girl from another village was frowned on in some parts of Derbyshire and the young man was forced to pay a fine to the males of the village where the girl lived. At Bradwell, this 'Cock Walk' fine was one shilling and sixpence but in most villages it was a shilling. In some places a round of

BRADWELL VILLAGE   *photo — Frank Rodgers*

drinks was accepted instead. If a boy refused to pay, he was paraded round the village with a rope round his neck.

Near most towns was a stretch of road known as the 'Bunny Run' or the 'Monkey Parade' where teenagers walked in twos or threes every Saturday or Sunday evening, hoping to 'click' with a member of the opposite sex and begin a regular 'walking out.'

Events leading up to courtship included the May Day frolics and 'going to the woods,' kissing games at Christmas time and village dances held in the local schoolroom, music being provided by the church organist at the piano. In those days, each dance, like the Lancers, lasted such a long time that it was said that the couples had time to become aquainted almost to the point of getting engaged before it came to an end.

Then there were the evening services at church or chapel, looked upon as social occasions at the beginning of this century, when girls hung about afterwards hoping to be invited to go for a walk. After three such walks with the same boy, the couple were recognised as 'keeping company.'

Strict parents limited 'courting nights' to no more than two or three a week and young people in domestic service were often allowed only one. The time fixed for returning home had to be rigidly adhered to or a punishment could be expected taking the form of a ban on further outings for some weeks, or, not infrequently, a 'good hiding' administered by an irate father.

SPOONING

One of the first indications that the association was becoming serious was 'spooning.' This meant sitting together on a garden wall or the bank of a stream while the boy carved a spoon for his sweetheart. Usually made of applewood, it was a true demonstration of the boy's devotion and honourable intentions. Symbols cut in the handle to indicate his affection showed a heart, a bird with a love message in its beak, or a key which denoted the sharing of a house. The bowl of the spoon was always kept plain and smooth ready to contain anything the girl might ask for.

When the boy was invited to the girl's home for tea on Sunday, it was a recognition of her parents' approval and was called in Derbyshire 'getting his feet under the table.' The visit also carried the privilege of occupying the parlour for an hour or two after tea. Often called the 'courting room,' this was the only occasion when a fire was lit there and many mothers insisted on the door being left open in order to prevent the couple 'getting too hot.' After the daughter married and left home, her mother was frequently heard to complain, 'our front room never gets aired these days,' for to light a fire in an unoccupied room was unthinkable.

If the girl belonged to a large family with a house full of younger brothers and sisters, there was little privacy and no spare room for courting. Liberal minded parents would therefore allow the girl's 'intended' to stay with her beside the kitchen fire after the rest of the family had retired to bed. After the couple had 'gone steady' for six months, it was thought permissible for them to spend the night together in the girl's bed, separated by a long pillow or a board.

BUNDLING

Called 'bundling' or 'bed-fellowship,' this was a long standing premarital custom in north Derbyshire until the end of the last century. The girl wore petticoats and the boy wore breeches and sometimes the girl's mother provided her daughter with a 'courting stocking,' made like pyjamas with one leg. But many parents considered no such precautions were necessary as the ability to conceive was thought to be more important than the preservation of virginity. Indeed, some families felt it expedient for the girl to prove that she was fertile before a wedding could be arranged.

'No baby, no wedding,' was a local saying.

If, as frequently occurred, the 'bundling' resulted in a pregnancy, the news was accepted with equanimity and jokes were made about the boy having 'jumped the bolster.'

This was one of many customs that met with strong disapproval from people living south of Chesterfield just as they despised the broader vowel sounds heard in that part of the county approaching Yorkshire. A young person using a coarse expression would be swiftly reprimanded with, 'We want none o' that sort o' talk here. We're not living in Sheffield.'

When 'bundling' was impossible because every bed in the house had too many occupants already, the couple had to seek solitude for their courting out of doors where they would discover secluded lanes and woodland paths and perhaps the shelter of a haystack for their lovemaking.

The middle class girl was more strictly chaperoned. She was never allowed to be alone with her 'young man' either indoors or outside until the engagement had been announced. Engagements could last many years before their combined savings justified the girl giving up her employment in order to get married when the two of them would have to live on one wage. Very few women went out to work after they were married.

Every girl who was engaged to be married had a 'bottom drawer' which she gradually filled with bed linen, table linen, kitchen utensils and anything for use in her future home. Sets of underclothes including chemises, camisoles and bloomers were hoarded, interspersed with little bags of lavender, until she had enough to last through a year of marriage.

Some village charities provided 'marriage portions' for 'poor and deserving brides' whose parents were unable to supply a dowry for them or even bear the cost of the wedding.

Wealthy parents supplied their daughters with sheets of real linen, tablecloths and napkins of damask, all embroidered with the bride's initials. These were stored in a carved wooden box with two drawers underneath which was known as a Dower Chest.

In upper class families where property and large amounts of money were involved, betrothals were often arranged for purposes of inheritance. It was a business transaction in which the bride's father provided the dowry and the husband a marriage settlement. Before agreeing to become the wife of the Earl of Shrewsbury, the ever resourceful Bess of Hardwick married her son to his daughter and her daughter to his son.

It was customary for children of the aristocracy to be betrothed at an early age, sometimes soon after birth, but in the 17th century this was restricted to the age of seven.

THE RING

The Romans introduced a formal betrothal ceremony in the presence of the two families concerned. Sacrifices were made to the goddess of marriage, Pronubia, and the man gave his intended wife an iron ring, signifying a pledge to marry. This was considered to be as binding as a wedding service and to break such a bond furnished grounds for compensation in Breach of Promise claims.

Over the centuries the betrothal ring changed from iron to gold or silver and, in the 19th century, girls liked to have a ring containing their birthstone. Later a multistone ring became fashionable. These rings were set with a number of different gems, every stone supposedly having an influence on the character of the girl who wore it.

Amethysts were said to keep extravagance at bay, acquamarines strengthened determination. Bloodstones imparted wisdom and forethought, diamonds increased willpower and emeralds safeguarded child-bearing. Garnets ensured loyalty and faithfulness and moonstones kept the thoughts pure. Opals were believed to reflect the mood of the wearer, pearls enhanced beauty and rubies promoted lightheartedness. Sapphires were for truth and sincerity and topazes were thought to induce a calm temperament. Turquoises could be expected to attract great wealth.

In late Victorian times the Harlequin ring was popular. This was composed of different stones, the initial letter of each spelling a word. A favourite combination was Amethyst, Moonstone, Opal, Ruby, Emerald, Topaz, giving 'AMORET,' meaning sweetheart, and sometimes the fiance's name, like George or Robert, was produced or just TOM with Topaz, Opal and Moonstone.

VALENTINE'S DAY

Valentine's Day, the time when birds were said to choose their partners, was the date for mating games to be played by young people, all with a view to finding out the identity of their future husbands. In the Glossop area boys put into a hat or a boot slips of paper with their names written on them. Each girl then drew a slip, noted the name and put it back. If she drew the same boy's name three times it was a sign that she would marry him before the next Valentine's day.

At Winster, girls wrote their names on pieces of paper which they then rolled up in pellets of clay. These were dropped into a pail of water and, when the clay dissolved, the papers rose to the surface. Each bachelor picked one out and was obliged to give the girl a present and a kiss.

Another Valentine custom was apple paring. A girl peeled an apple in one long piece then threw this over her left shoulder on to the ground where it was supposed to form the initial of her prospective bridegroom.

On the night before Valentine's day, Derby girls boiled an egg hard, removed the yolk and filled the cavity with salt. They then ate the yolkless egg, salt and all, without speaking at bedtime and hoped on waking, to see their future husbands.

Valentine cards were popular in the 19th century and sales have revived since the Second World War. Formerly, they were always delivered, secretly, by hand at the girl's house after dark. Decorated with flowers, ribbons or love-birds, they often contained original but terrible rhymes, sometimes in the form of a proposal of marriage.

'With this card my heart I'm sending,
Love for you is never ending,
If you consent to be my bride,
My longing heart will swell with pride.'

Midsummer Eve was also the occasion for a girl to catch a glimpse of the man she would marry. Running round the parish church at midnight, she threw hempseed over her shoulder, reciting as she ran,

'Hempseed I throw, Hempseed I sow,
He that is my true love come after me and mow.'

At the twelfth circuit her future husband was supposed to appear before her, momentarily, as a wraith.

It is said that a girl at Eckington lost count of the number of times she had run round the church and fell down in a dead faint. On recovering, she insisted that she had lost consciousness not on account of exhaustion but because she was confronted by a man she detested and would rather die than marry. She died shortly afterwards.

ECKINGTON CHURCH *photo — Frank Rodgers*

LEONARD WHEATCROFT'S WOOING

Leonard Wheatcroft of Ashover, born in 1627, who became Parish Clerk, Schoolmaster and Landlord of the 'Hand and Shears' in that village, wrote his autobiography in a manuscript of 24 pages, each measuring 5 inches by 3 inches. He describes a succession of affairs of the heart during which he addressed his current lady-love in poetry.

The lovely Frances Smith of Higham, on account of her father's disapproval, was forced to 'sparre the doore' on him, causing him to lament,

'Sometimes I walk into the fieldes
My love for to restraine,
But that to me small comforte yields
For all is still in vaine.'

After dallying for a time with Anne Newton, a local girl, he began to make excursions on horseback to Winster to see Elizabeth Hawley which continued for two years.

'And if you would know how many times I went a-wooing,' he wrote 'you shall find so many slashes upon an ash tree at Winster Towne Ende, and how many miles I have travelled for her sake — they were 400 and 40 and odd.'

After many love letters to his 'sweet Betty,' he penned her a proposal.

'My joy and dearest love, My penne, my hande, my love, my sword, my life and all I have are ready to be employed at your commande.'

They were married on 20th May 1657.

WEDDINGS

'I have always thought that every woman should marry but no man,' wrote Benjamin Disraeli in the 18th century.

In Anglo-Saxon times fathers disposed of their daughters to the highest bidder. The transaction was on the 'on approval' basis and they could be exchanged if they failed to give satisfaction. The agreed sum of money, known as the 'wed,' was handed over in church. After the vows were made, the bridegroom removed one of his bride's shoes and hit her over the head with it. This signified that he was now her master and was the origin of a shoe being tied to the honeymoon vehicle.

DROIT DE SEIGNEUR

Under the ancient manorial system, permission from the feudal lord had to be obtained before any of his vassals could get married and this was only reluctantly given if the proposed bride or groom lived in another village.

It was customary for the lord to take advantage of his established right, the 'droit de seigneur,' to deflower the bride on the night before the wedding. If a child was born nine months afterwards, there was much speculation about its paternity.

Because too many young people were joined in what came to be called 'Holy Deadlock', a law was passed in 1556 to raise the age of completing an apprenticeship to twenty-four. Consequently, craftsmen could not afford to marry before that age and weddings of younger men took place only when the bridegroom was a member of the upper classes.

From that time until the end of the century, the average age of marriage for women was 25 to 26 years but this was older than it sounds because of the length of life expectancy compared with today.

WEDDING SEASONS.

The traditional ruling as to when a wedding could or could not take place originated in the church's ban on sexual relations during certain seasons of the ecclesiastical year.

> *'Advent bids thee to containe,*
> *Hilarie sets thee free againe,*
> *Septuagesima says thee nay,*
> *Eight days from Easter and you may.*
> *Ascension pleads for chastitie*
> *Yet thou mayst wed at Trinitie.'*

Because weddings were banned in Lent, Easter was a popular time to get married. May, always considered an unlucky month was consistently avoided.

> *'Marry in May, you'll rue the day.'*

June was a favourite month and so were October and November when harvest time had come to an end and wages had been paid for the year of service. In farming districts, December was avoided for a Christmas wedding was likely to produce a summer pregnancy (tiresome during the hot weather) and a lying-in in September or October when farm life was busiest.

THE WEDDING DAY

'Marry on Monday, marry for health,
Marry on Tuesday, marry for wealth,
Marry on Wednesday, best day of all.
Marry on Thursday, marry for losses,
Marry on Friday, marry for crosses,
Marry on Saturday, no luck at all.'

Saturday has now become the most popular day for a wedding but earlier this century most village weddings were celebrated on a Sunday, the only day in the week when both bride and bridegroom had a holiday. There were no half days either on Saturday or during the week.

BANNS

Until the beginning of this century, a man was prohibited from marrying his deceased wife's sister, his deceased brother's wife and many non-blood relations listed in the Book of Common Prayer. These were among the 'just causes or impediments' referred to when the Banns of Marriage were read at Morning Prayer on three 'several Sundays' before the wedding.

After the publication of banns by the clergyman, the Parish Clerk would rise and say, 'God speed them well,' and the congregation added, 'Amen.'

Many prospective brides still refuse to attend the service at which their own banns are called on account of an old superstition that, if they do so, their children will be born deaf and dumb.

GOING TO CHURCH

Unless the bride and groom lived some distance away, they both walked to church from their respective homes. The bride hoped to see a black cat, a grey horse or a chimney sweep on the way to bring her good luck but if anyone accidentally trod on her shadow, she could expect to die within a year. So upset was a girl at Bakewell when this occurred as she was passing through the churchyard, that she returned home and refused to be married that day. To see an open grave on the way was believed to predict a death in the family so the bride would be led past it with her eyes closed.

Until the 19th century, working class brides rarely had attendants but were preceded on the walk to church by a young girl strewing blossoms and petals on the road before her.

REPTON CHURCH   *photo — Frank Rodgers*

At one time in north east Derbyshire, the bride was escorted to church by two bachelors and walked home after the service with two married men. Similarly, the groom was attended by two unmarried girls on the way to church and, on his return, walked between two married women. This practice was continued in villages round Bolsover until the First World War.

Weddings were always arranged to take place on the hour but neither bride nor bridegroom would go into church before the clock struck for it was unlucky to hear it strike during the service. By tradition, the groom entered on the last stroke allowing the bride to arrive ten minutes later for it was unlucky for him to see her until she joined him in church. He was careful not to turn to watch her walk up the aisle as this was unlucky too.

THE WEDDING DRESS

During the reign of Elizabeth the First it became customary for well-to-do people to provide a marriage feast for their servants, stipulating that 'the maydens about to marrie must be pure.' For this reason brides began to wear white to confirm their virginity.

At the beginning of the 19th century, few brides wore veils but lace trimmed caps, bonnets or floral hats were set upon hair styles which, at that time, grew higher and higher. The white dress continued to be popular and, later, the bridal outfit included a wreath and veil together with a bouquet. Raising the veil at the end of the ceremony was symbolic of becoming a wife. It was thought lucky to wear a veil belonging to somebody who was happily married.

'Something old, something new, something borrowed and something blue,' to be included in the bride's ensemble has been a tradition for generations. The 'something blue' in the 17th century was usually her garters which became trophies to be worn in the hats of the young men who succeeded in stripping them from her legs, sometimes before she left the altar.

THE SERVICE

There has been little variation in the marriage service since the 14th century when the bridegroom undertook to 'haven and holden for fayrer for fouler' and the bride promised to be 'bonlich and buxom (meek and obliging) in bed and at borde.'

There was an unwritten law at one time which declared that if a man married a woman 'en chemisette,' that is, in her underclothes, he could not be made responsible for her debts.

It is said that a middle aged Repton woman turned up at church for her wedding wearing only a petticoat and, equally indecent, nothing upon her head. This was according to the conditions laid down by the man she was going to marry.

THE WEDDING RING

Wedding rings have not always been worn continually. At one time a borrowed ring was used for the church ceremony and many brides did not come into possession of one of their own until their mother or mother-in-law passed away. Then the bride would inherit her wedding ring.

The ring is placed on the third finger of the bride's left hand as this finger is supposed to contain a vein carrying blood directly to the heart.

A catastrophe is foreshadowed if the ring falls to the floor during the service.

A couple being married at Hope early in the last century stood before the vicar making their vows. The bridegroom was on the point of placing the ring on the bride's finger when the cry of hounds in pursuit of a fox was heard. Dropping the ring back in his pocket, the man ran out of the church and joined the hunt. No record has been preserved of the bride's reaction to his behaviour but it is said that the couple appeared at church next day and the ceremony was continued.

FERTILITY RITES

Outside church, after the service, today's bride and groom are showered with confetti and this is a relic of an old fertility rite. Childbearing was originally the main reason for getting married so it was customary to throw figs (because of their many seeds), rice and nuts (plenty of nuts, plenty of cradles) over the newly married pair. At some places in the Peak District, including Castleton and Stoney Middleton, they were pelted with sods in addition to the grain. This was for luck in the produce of the soil as well as for a good number of offspring.

At this point, the bride was supposed to throw her bouquet to the crowd of guests, the one to catch it being the next to get married according to an old prophecy. A sprig from the bride's bouquet, myrtle being the favourite, was often taken by the best man and planted in some garden as a gift from the bride.

In north Derbyshire children used to shut and fasten the church gates after the bridal party had gone into church. The bridegroom was then expected to throw them pennies in the form of a toll before he and his bride were allowed to pass through.

SHOWING THE MARRIED COUPLE

If funds permitted, a conveyance was hired in which the bride and groom with their attendants drove through the village after the service in order to show themselves to the parishioners. At several places they would find a rope stretched across the road where they had to pay a toll before the whole party was plied with drinks.

Called 'Showing the married couple,' this was a typically Peak District custom remembered by people alive today who also recall that the driver often imbibed to such an extent that it was left to his horse (the only sober one in the party) to return them safely to the bride's home for the reception.

THE RECEPTION

Centuries ago a 'Bride Ale' took place in church immediately after the service. Guests were supplied with food and drink and expected to make monetary contributions to the bridal couple. In the 18th and 19th centuries 'Penny Weddings' grew more and more popular, each guest handing over a gift of money not exceeding an amount stated beforehand, usually five shillings.

The father of a bride at Clay Cross, however, insisted that theirs must be a true Penny Wedding and nothing more than a single penny from each guest was accepted.

Later the celebrations took place in a nearby hall where singing, dancing and games were enjoyed and so the wedding reception was established.

For the poorer classes, wedding receptions were often frugal, affairs, in no way comparable to the lavish provisions following a funeral. The bride's mother rarely attended the church service but stayed at home to prepare the wedding 'breakfast,' so-called at whatever time of day the meal took place. It was not unusual for the groom, if he were an agricultural labourer, to have a quick bite and return to work.

THE WEDDING CAKE

The Romans crumbled a simple wheat cake over the head of the bride after the wedding service. This was a fertility rite to ensure good fortune in childbearing.

It was in Charles I's reign that the French custom of having cakes specially made for weddings was introduced into England. A rich fruit cake was made for the groom and a light sponge cake decorated with sugar for the bride.

Several hundred years later the three tier cake became fashionable, the largest tier at the bottom being eaten at the reception, the middle one cut up and sent to absent friends and the top one saved for the first christening.

Superstition ruled that the bride should not taste the cake beforehand and that she must cut it with her husband's help or she would remain childless.

Unmarried girls placed a piece of wedding cake under their pillows in the belief that they would dream of their future husbands as a result.

BEDDING THE MARRIED COUPLE

Wherever the reception was held it was customary for the guests to gather at the bridal couple's new home for the 'Bedding Ceremony.' They crowded into the bedroom where they drank toasts in possets made with hot wine then, having helped the bride and bridegroom to bed, they continued the celebrations downstairs. Someone, previously, tied a bell underneath the nuptial bed so that every movement was registered and greeted with a rousing cheer.

Before departing, every guest, together with the clergyman who had officiated at the wedding, was presented with a pair of gloves.

When honeymoons became popular, the practice of 'bedding the couple' gradually disappeared.

YOUTH AND AGE

At Sheldon in the High Peak a wedding was solemnised in 1753 when a bride was a widow of about eighty and the bridegroom a lad of fourteen who was marrying with the consent (and probably the encouragement) of his parents.

The bride was carried to church on a chair and after the service to a celebration dance at which she beat time with her hands. The same ritual took place as that following an ordinary wedding. The guests were admitted to the bedroom, the couple were bedded and toasts to them were drunk in all seriousness.

The bride did not live long afterwards.

CIVIL CONTRACT

During the Commonwealth period weddings in church were banned altogether and marriage became a purely civil contract made before a Justice of the Peace.

The diary of Leonard Wheatcroft of Ashover contains details of his wedding to Elizabeth Hawley in 1657. The church bells in 'Asher' rang out as friends with flying colours attached to their wrists accompanied Leonard to Winster to fetch his bride. Under Puritan rules church weddings were banned so the wedding party journeyed to Brackenfield where Leonard and Elizabeth were married by Mr. Justice Spateman at his house. They returned to Ashover for the bridal dinner when many became intoxicated.

'Far into the night,' wrote Leonard, 'they got us into bed with no small adoe.'

In spite of Oliver Cromwell's law, weddings continued to take place, surreptitiously, in church but were conducted with such secrecy that a contemporary writer commented on the number of women 'brought to bed of legitimate children without anyone having heard a word of their fathers.'

After the Restoration when church weddings were allowed once more, it became the fashion to marry in secret or to elope. Having reached Gretna Green, couples could be married instantly without parental consent and, by the end of the 17th century, Derbyshire had its own Gretna Green.

PEAK FOREST

In 1657 Christiana, Duchess of Devonshire, built a chapel at Peak Forest in memory of 'Charles, King and Martyr' and this began to be called the 'English Gretna Green.' A free chapelry, outside the jurisdiction of the bishop, its vicar had the arbitrary rights to perform wedding ceremonies and issue marriage licences at any time of the day or night.

A special register was kept for 'foreign' weddings (couples not of the county of Derby) and the chapel became so well known that in the year 1745 no fewer than 105 such marriages were solemnised there.

In 1748 a wealthy young couple eloped from Scotland and made their way on horseback to be married at Peak Forest. Spending the night at the Royal Oak Inn at Stoney Middleton, the bride-to-be dreamed that she saw her future husband murdered. Next day they paused for a while at an inn at Castleton where their well-to-do appearance was noticed by a group of local ruffians. Having left Castleton for Peak Forest, the couple were waylaid in the lonely Winnats Pass and hacked to death with a pickaxe. Their skeletons, buried in a sack, were discovered ten years later.

WINNATS PASS

photo — Frank Rodgers

The identity of the murderers might never have come to light if one of the four, all miners, had not confessed to the crime on his death bed.

By an act of Parliament in 1804, marriages at Peak Forest Chapel were made illegal on account of 'being productive of bad consequences.'

The chapel was demolished in the 1870's but even today couples can be married in the church at Peak Forest without banns having been previously called. The only stipulation is that one of them must have been resident in the village for at least fifteen days.

DOROTHY VERNON

Derbyshire's most famous story of an elopement is that of Dorothy Vernon who, in Tudor times, escaped from her home, Haddon Hall, and rode away with John Manners, son of the Earl of Rutland. It is said that the first night of their elopement was spent at the Red Cow Inn, Allestree.

'In Allestrey on the outskirts of Derby they paused,' wrote an essayist. 'Gold procured refreshment, two fresh horses and a side-saddle for Dorothy. The morning mists were rising as they passed through Derby on their way to Aylestone where they married.'

A MOCK MARRIAGE

A Derbyshire story has been handed down concerning the

MINERS ARMS, EYAM   *photo — Frank Rodgers*

marriage of a rector of Eyam, the Reverend Joseph Hunt. After baptising a baby belonging to one of his parishoners, Matthew Ferns who was landlord of the Miners Arms, the rector was invited to join in the merrymaking that followed.

More than a little drunk, Joseph began to make advances to Matthew's eighteen year old daughter, Anne. Producing a book of Common Prayer, he went through the Solemnisation of Holy Matrimony ceremony with her, conducted by one of the guests and witnessed by the whole gathering.

When the news of this affair reached the Bishop of Derby, he insisted thet Mr. Hunt should marry the girl in the proper manner which he did on September 4th 1684.

A young lady to whom he had been engaged, however, sued him for Breach of Promise, causing him 'to become deeply in debt. Obliged to leave the rectory, he and his wife made their abode in the church vestry, thereby avoiding his creditors. Here they spent the remainder of their married life and brought up two children.

MARRIAGE

When a Saxon woman got married, her kinsmen continued to keep a watch on the treatment she received from her husband ensuring that her social status was maintained and she was often allowed to own property in her own right which was more than an 18th or 19th century wife could do.

Saxon women fought in battle together with their husbands. Ethelfleda, widow of the Lord of Mercia which included Derbyshire, became a military leader like Boadicea and led her troops on horseback, conquering the Danes and capturing Derby for the Saxons. Tradition has it that, in gratitude, she built the first Saint Mary's Bridge over the River Derwent in Derby.

In Feudal times a wife was regarded as one of her husband's 'goods and chattels' and she held no rights or possessions of her own. She was not allowed to bear witness in the case of murder unless the murdered man was her husband.

The main role of a wife in those days was in producing children and the most shaming situation she could find herself in was her inability to breed. For this, like giving birth to daughters instead of sons, she was held entirely to blame. Whatever the class of society, it was important to have a son for the eldest male child inherited whatever his father possessed even, in the case of a peasant, his animals, tools and the tenancy of his holding or cottage.

The latter would consist of a single room with a floor of earth where the whole family lived, slept and ate. In the bitter winter weather small animals such as pigs and goats were brought inside, partly for their own protection from the cold and partly for the warmth they contributed to the human inhabitants.

Most peasant women spent their whole lives in the manor or village where they were born; indeed they needed the Lord of the Manor's permission to move away. Cottages often accommodated three generations although, because of the shorter span of life, there were fewer elderly people than there are today. Grandmothers could mind the babies, keep an eye on the pot over the fire and mend clothes. Grandfathers were useful for feeding the animals and watching livestock that was inclined to stray.

It was so unusual for a woman to live alone that any one doing so was suspected of being a witch.

During the MIDDLE AGES, King Henry II became very concerned for the safety of women in his realm. One of his strict laws on social behaviour ruled that any man who forced a woman to have sexual intercourse against her will should be castrated.

During the Crusades when women were left to run whole estates, supervising the workpeople and selling produce and livestock, a departing husband would leave his wife locked in a chastity belt. In this situation, rape was impossible but it was done mainly on account of the fear that the man's lands and inheritance might pass to an illegitimate child of his wife. In the absence of a legal heir, however, it was not unusual for a bastard son of the husband to be acknowledged and inherit accordingly.

After the Crusades, homes became more comfortable for men brought from the East not only seeds and plants such as the snowdrop for their gardens but carpets, bedcovers and cushions which housewives welcomed with delight.

Trade increased at this time and thus developed a new social class between landowners and peasants known as the MIDDLE CLASS. Women, however, were strongly discouraged from aspiring to a higher grade of society and condemned for copying the dress of their superiors. In fact, a law was passed in 1285 forbidding any woman not of the upper classes to go out of doors wearing 'a hood furred with other than lambskin or rabbitskin.'

In spite of rules about their headgear, the position of these women gradually improved, many becoming independent like Chaucer's 'Wife of Bath' who had 'enjoyed five husbands' and travelled on several pilgrimages. But, in spite of their new prosperity, women were still underprivileged citizens compared with their husbands.

After the Black Death swept through Derbyshire carrying off one third of the population, women confined themselves to work in the house and the dairy and looking after the production of poultry and eggs which they sold at markets. A status symbol for a housewife at this time was a boy walking behind her on the way to market, carrying the produce she had for sale and, on the way back, carrying her baskets full of purchases. At the same time he acted as a protector against assailants.

The BOKE OF HUSBANDRY, written by a Derbyshire man in 1523, set forth a routine of work expected of a yeoman's wife in that era. The author's name on the fly leaf of this book was Master Fitzherbert which might have been Anthony or his brother, John. Both lived at the Old Manor House at Norbury which was occupied by a succession of members of the Fitzherbert family and it is probable that the book was written there.

'First sweep thy house,' it directs, 'dress up thy dishboard, milk thy kye, suckle thy calves, sye up thy milk, take up thy children and array them and provide for thy husband's breakfast, dinner, supper and for thy children and servants. Ordain corn and malt to the mill, bake and brew when the need is, make butter and cheese, serve thy swine both morning and evening and give thy poultry meat in the morning. At the beginning of Spring, make thy garden,

OLD MANOR HOUSE, NORBURY   *photo — Frank Rodgers*

getting as many seeds and herbs as be good for the pot and to eat.'

An added, one would have thought unnecessary, exhortation comes at the end.

'Let thy distaff always be ready for a pastime that thou be not idle.'

In enumerating the good points to look for when buying a horse, Master Fitzherbert likened some of these to qualities desirable in a wife.

'To have broade buttockes . . . to be easy to leape upon . . . to be well sturrynge under a man.'

In COMMONWEALTH times, life was drab and joyless and women were condemned for attempting to make themselves attractive. All finery and ornaments were banned, sober coloured clothes were the rule and even wives who did no housework were expected to cover themselves in plain white aprons.

After the RESTORATION, entertainments were revived and entertaining again became popular with invitations to 'take a dish of tea,' the new beverage.

Samuel Pepys's diary, begun in 1660, gives an insight into the lives of a middle class family. His household consisted of 'My wife in good health; her woman, Mercer; her chambermaid, Besse; her cook-maid, Jane; the little girl, Susan, and my boy, Tom Edwards.' On one occasion when they were entertaining friends, he wrote, 'My poore wife rose by five o'clock in the morning, before day, and went to market and bought fowles and many things for dinner.'

In the 18th century middle class women did less and less housework themselves, leaving all chores to their servants and, like Jane Austen's characters, spending their time in letter writing, visiting and, for short periods only, overlooking the upbringing of their children.

The extended family, common since Medieval times, continued with many houses accommodating three generations, the wife's position often being made stressful by an overbearing grandparent or sister-in-law. Any relative, single or widowed, took for granted their welcome in the house of a brother or a sister.

Poorer people's homes at this time were little better than those in the Middle Ages and working class wives were just as overburdened with constant childbearing and rearing large families.

Workhouses were built for those unable to support themselves or without relations to do so but conditions in them were appalling and the death rate of children was alarmingly high. One of the first workhouses in Derbyshire was situated in the Osmaston Road, Derby, and was locally known as 'The Bastille.'

STEPMOTHERS

Many orphans were condemned to a workhouse upbringing for mothers frequently died in childbirth. Worn out with hard work, a lack of nourishing food and a succession of pregnancies with inexpert attention, they succumbed easily, leaving a husband with a number of children on his hands. It was not unusual to find a girl of twelve or thirteen having to take on the responsibility of household duties and the care of her young brothers and sisters.

Many widowers lost no time in looking for a substitute mother for their offspring, the bride being chosen for her suitability in coping with a family rather than for an attractive appearance or personality.

Some of the cruel stepmother stories are not without foundation. If not deliberately unkind, some of these women were often insensitive, many of them spiteful in the treatment of their stepchildren who spent an unhappy childhood as a result.

It was not only the lower classes who suffered in this way. Dorothy Vernon of Haddon Hall is said to have encountered difficulties with her stepmother. Only a few years older than Dorothy and her sister, Maud Longford had married Sir George Vernon because of family pressure. She found happiness only when he died and she was free to marry the man of her choice.

The fifteen year old Elizabeth Strutt was left, after her mother's death, in sole charge of the household while her father, Jedediah, was away from home for long periods. When he remarried, the family were so unfriendly towards their stepmother that he left them in occupation of the house in St. Peter's Street, Derby, and settled with his bride at Milford near one of his mills.

One Derbyshire notable who managed to find a capable step-mother for his large family was Anthony Bradshaw of Duffield. His two wives, between them, produced twenty-three children.

DISORDERLY CONDUCT

Any kind of misbehaviour, particularly on the part of a wife living in a small village, was difficult to conceal and the culprit was often exposed to 'Rough Music.' Villagers would gather at night round the offender's house banging pots and pans and shouting insulting rhymes. At Belper they did not hesitate to break the windows and throw turds through them.

An assortment of contraptions was invented over the years

for the restraint of tiresome women. A female of loose morals inclined to unseemly conduct was tied to a Ducking Stool placed in front of her house where she was open to public derision. The Tumbrel was a kind of chair fixed to a cart on which the woman was pulled round the village, receiving jeers, rotten eggs and mud thrown at her. The Ducking Stool was fastened to the end of a plank which swivelled round, plunging the victim into a pond or river.

The Branks or Scold's Bridle was popular in the 17th century, one being kept at Chesterfield and other towns for the punishment of women using abusive or obscene language. Constructed like a horse's bridle, it fitted over the woman's head and had a piece of sharp metal which cut her tongue if it moved. It was loaned to any husband who suffered from a persistently nagging wife.

THE QUIET WOMAN

In the little Derbyshire village of Earl Sterndale is an inn called 'The Quiet Woman.' The sign over the door depicts a headless woman and underneath is the inscription, 'Soft Words turneth away wrath.' One explanation recounts that the landlady at the inn was such an incessant talker that not only her husband but the customers became exhausted by the sound of her voice. When she began to talk continually in her sleep, her husband could stand it no longer and he cut off her head.

THE QUIET WOMAN INN   *photo — J. Mellor*

DIVORCE

Before 1870 a husband could take possession of all his wife's earnings and, until 1879, he was allowed to beat his wife without showing justification for so doing. Before 1882, he owned all his wife's belongings — clothes, jewellery, money or any property she had inherited from a member of her family. Before 1891, a husband could lock up his wife as a punishment for her misdeeds, even though she protested innocence, and, until 1920, the home and lands comprising an estate were always in the husband's name even though the wife had brought them into the marriage.

Before the first Divorce Court opened in 1857, the only way to obtain a divorce was by means of a special Act of Parliament costing approximately £3,000. Unfaithfulness in marriage was regarded as excusable in a man but unforgivable in a woman and, whereas a man could divorce his wife on the grounds of adultery alone, a woman had to prove adultery with another cause or causes in addition. Divorced wives were considered unsuitable to bring up the children of the marriage and it was almost automatic for the husband to be given custody.

Double standards were employed for men and women in the assessment of marriage settlements until the latter half of this century. The 5th Duke of Devonshire fathered at least three illegitimate children, one of them being born about the time of his marriage to the beautiful Lady Georgiana Spencer and he had two others by Lady Elizabeth Foster who became part of the 'menage à trois' at Chatsworth and married the duke after Georgiana died. Georgiana, on the other hand, bore a child, the result of a brief affair with Charles Grey who later became Prime Minister, and she was banished to live abroad.

WIFE SELLING

Poorer people resorted to wife selling. There was an unwritten law, prevalent in Derbyshire, that a man could lawfully sell his wife provided that he delivered her to the purchaser with a halter round her neck. Accordingly, many wives were taken to market in this manner and paraded round the market square, the husband extolling her good points in a loud voice or sometimes paying the Town Crier to do it for him. She was then auctioned and sold to the highest bidder.

On 5th December 1772, Thomas Bott sold his wife on Derby market place to a man from Langley Common for 18d (7½pence) which was said to be an average price. The sale was completed over drinks at a nearby inn in the presence of many onlookers. Some years later a man sold his wife at the market at Chesterfield in exchange for a sheepdog and a bale of hay.

THE VICTORIAN AGE

Overcrowding was one of the worst features of Victorian life. In industrial towns, women had to cope with smoky back to back houses or tenements and sometimes lived in cellars. Every drop of water had to be carried from a communal well or pump, often some distance away from the dwelling and one outside privy was shared with several other families. Children slept five or six to a bed for the average number of children in a family was six, not taking into account the number who died. At mealtimes, they ate standing up or else sitting on a doorstep.

Wives in Derbyshire mining villages waited in their backyards for husbands coming off the 'shift.' Swilling coal dust from the men's heads and necks before allowing them into the house, they were careful to avoid wetting their backs for colliers believed that this would weaken them and cause them to become unfit for work in the pit.

A working man's wage was abysmally low and a large proportion of it was often spent in the alehouse. After sustained drinking sessions, husbands frequently physically abused their wives and terrified their children.

GIN

The struggle to make ends meet in attempting to keep a large family fed and clothed imposed years of hardship on the mothers who, at this time, began to drown their desperation in gin.

'Drunk for a penny, dead drunk for twopence,' said the

advertisements and gin was sold, without a licence, at all the little corner shops. In the towns it was a common sight to see women lying, gin-drunk, in doorways or jennels, oblivious to rain or falling snow.

PAWNSHOPS

A large proportion of the money used for the purchase of gin came from the pawnshops. These 'hock-shops' as they were called in some parts of Derbyshire, with their three golden balls, were now springing up in increasing numbers and played an important part in the lives of downtrodden Victorian women.

Father's suit, if he had one, or his Sunday jacket, together with Mother's best bonnet and shawl, a piece of jewellery of any value or even a wedding ring, was 'popped' on Monday morning to be redeemed on payday, the procedure being repeated week after week. Naturally, from time to time, it was impossible to find the necessary money with which to reclaim the articles pledged and so they were lost for ever.

All but the very poor, however, took a pride in their homes, keeping them spick and span and dressing the table legs in stockings to prevent scratching from cats' claws. For each day of the week they allotted a household chore, eyeing with contempt a neighbour who diverged from the routine. Washday, which was customarily Monday unless altered for some good reason, presented the most difficulties for drying clothes in wet weather caused infinite discomfort.

> Those who wash on Monday have all the week to dry,
> Those who wash on Tuesday are not so much awry,
> Those who wash on Wednesday one hesitates to blame
> But those who wash on Thursday wash for very shame.
> Those who wash on Friday, wash in need
> And those who wash on Saturday are sluts indeed.

No mention is made of washing on Sunday. In all classes of society, that would be unthinkable. Even to hang out a baby's nappy on the Sabbath would be inviting the wrath of the Almighty.

Few lower middle class families, in these times, were unable to afford at least one servant. Called the 'maid of all work,' this girl was reputedly badly treated, badly fed and made to sleep in a cold, dark attic.

At the other end of the social scale, it was not uncommon for a single establishment to employ between twenty and thirty indoor and outdoor staff including a nanny and a governess.

FIRST WORLD WAR

These circumstances continued until the First World war when there was a scarcity of domestic servants on account of the number of women employed in war work. Shortages of food meant that mothers had to stand queueing with babies or young children for hours in order to supply their families with a reasonable diet.

Country people had the advantage (if they were not caught) of being able to poach game or even make a meal of a few netted singing birds and everyone in the New Tupton area knew about the woman who had skinned and cooked a cat and dished it up for her husband's dinner, disguised as a rabbit.

The GREAT DEPRESSION which followed caused extensive unemployment, in some areas eighty-five per cent of a town's population subsisting on the 'dole.' Badly hit were the mining villages of Derbyshire where unemployed colliers could be seen, day after day, sitting by the roadsides, some of them rocking a baby in a pram, some passing a cigarette from one to another for 'a couple of draws' each.

Wives were said to encourage their menfolk to stay in bed until noon in order to save the cost of breakfast, for their weekly pay on the Means Test was quite inadequate to provide food and warmth and clothing. It merely prevented outright starvation.

TODAY'S WOMAN

During and after the Second World War, a woman's position in society changed dramatically. Formerly, where women, on marrying, were banned from many professions, they were now welcomed as equal to men. Married women today are in command of their own incomes whether earned or unearned for the greatest change of all has been the increase in the number of wives and mothers who go out to work.

The attitude to marriage has altered considerably but an old piece of Derbyshire advice to both brides and bridegrooms is still applicable today.

'Keep your eyes wide open before you are married but half shut afterwards.'

Death, Burial and Memorials

DEATH

'If life were a thing that money could buy,
The poor could not live and the rich would not die.'

Since the Second World War death and bereavement have become as unmentionable as sex in Victorian times. Nevertheless, there is still a widespread belief in those superstitions, mostly of a pagan origin, which foretell an approaching death.

SIGNS AND PORTENTS

'A green Christmas makes a fat churchyard,' is a national saying and Derbyshire people believe that mild weather in any part of December will be followed by a large number of deaths in January.

A dog howling during the night, a cock crowing after dusk has fallen or a robin chirping close by a house are all thought to be warnings of a death occurring in the area where the sound was heard. The ticking of the death-watch beetle has always put fear into the hearts of those who heard it for, like the sound of fingers tapping on a table or an unexplained knocking on the wall of a house, it is taken as a premonition of death.

A crow, bird of ill-omen, perching on a house roof was believed to foretell the death of someone living there and a crow seen in a churchyard indicated a funeral.

The feathers of a peacock taken into a house could mean death for one of the occupants and, if bees forsook their hives, it was a sign that their owner would shortly die.

A white butterfly entering a room at night was looked upon as a harbinger of death and, if a bird flew into a sick room, it was said to be seeking the soul of the invalid which would leave the body as soon as death took place.

Anyone seeing a coke shoot out from a burning fire would inspect it carefully to discover if it resembled a cradle or a coffin. Shaped like the latter, a death in the house could be expected.

People living in north Derbyshire have always been reluctant to chop down thorn trees, terrifying tales having been passed down concerning tragedies that followed the felling of a thorn tree. Hawthorn blossoms taken into a house were often held responsible for a fatal illness.

> '*Hawthorn bloom and elder flowers*
> *Fill the house with evil powers.*'

Flowers that hang their heads like bluebells and violets and especially those with a sweet smell were thought to bring bad luck if taken indoors. Scented lilac, particularly the white variety, has always been associated with death.

WATCHING THE CHURCH

There was once a belief that, on Saint Mark's Eve, April 24th, all those who were going to die in the following year

DRONFIELD CHURCH   *photo — Frank Rodgers*

would pass through the churchyard and into the church. A man at Dronfield was said to have kept watch, year after year, in the porch of Saint John the Baptist's church there but he saw no sign of a ghostly procession and attempted to reassure the parishioners that such a visitation did not take place. But few people believed him and every year children continued to 'Watch the Church,' usually in the hope of some excitement or for a 'dare.' Older people said they preferred not to know who was going to die.

DEATHBED CONFESSIONS

It is said that a dying man will not take his last breath until he has disclosed a guilty secret which has been on his mind for a long time. This was the case of the Derbyshire miner who took part in the assassination of a young couple in the Winnats Pass in 1748 as they were on their way to be married at Peak Forest Chapel, the local Gretna Green. He confessed to his share of the murder on his deathbed.

THE PASSING BELL

'When the bell begins to toll,
Lord have mercy on his soul.'

As someone lay dying all locks and bolts securing doors and windows in the house were drawn in order to 'ease the passing' and, when it was certain that death was approaching, a message was sent to the sexton who rang the church bell.

Known as the Passing Bell, it was rung, originally, to call the priest to offer prayers at the bedside of the one whose life was departing. It was also believed to frighten away any demons who might be waiting to capture the spirit when it left the body. Its tolling was a signal to parishioners that one of their members was about to leave this world. Usually a tenor bell was used for the passing of an adult and a treble bell for a child.

Varying from place to place, there was a recognised number of tolls which denoted the dying person's sex and age. At Horsley and Holbrook the bell was rung three times for a man and twice for a woman, in the High Peak it was seven for a man and five for a woman but, elsewhere in Derbyshire, the sexton would ring nine strokes for a man, six for a woman and three for a child. Each stroke was called 'teller,' corrupted in some places to 'tailor,' hence the ringing of 'Nine Tailors.' After a short pause, a single stroke was rung for each year of the dying person's age.

'Seventy-eight,' muttered an old man in Alfreton as he lay in bed counting the strokes. ''Tis for me. I'll show 'em.' And he got himself out of bed and shook his fist through the open window. But the exertion must have hastened his end for he was dead within an hour.

In the 19th century the DEPARTING BELL began to be tolled after death instead of during the passing and now it rings only when the funeral is about to take place.

For centuries the funeral bell of All Saints, Derby, was tolled, free of charge, for everyone buried there but at Chesterfield, until 1788, two shillings was charged for 'those who require the great bell on the occasion of a burial.' Paupers had to be content with the tolling of a smaller bell.

DRAWING THE PILLOW

If, like King Charles II, someone took 'an unconscionable time a-dying,' then it was considered permissible to hasten the end by smartly pulling the pillow from beneath the dying person's head, making him fall backwards with a jerk.

THE CORPSE

Immediately after death, all mirrors in the house were covered over and every clock was stopped. It was said that many clocks, particularly the grandfather type, stopped of their own accord at the time of their owner's death. They were not made to start again until after the funeral. This was supposed to prevent another death occurring in the house.

If the eyes of a corpse remained open after death, it was taken as a sign that he was looking for another to join him in the churchyard and a further death could be expected.

LAYING OUT

In every village there was at least one woman accustomed

to laying out a dead body and she was sent for as quickly as possible. Tying a bandage round the head to hold the jaw firmly in place and placing pennies over the eyes to keep them closed, she then straightened the limbs, usually leaving the hands crossed on the chest.

According to custom, all cloths used in washing the body were burned and the woman was given a drink of whisky or brandy to 'take away the taste of death' which, otherwise, was said to linger for days. The customary fee for this service was half-a-crown.

LYCH-WAKING

The undertaker, having brought the coffin, wrapped the body in a shroud before placing it therein. Until 1666 linen shrouds were commonly used although a woman was often buried in her best nightdress. An Act of Parliament in that year, however, ruled that all corpses should be wrapped in wool in order to support the English woollen trade.

The open coffin was left, usually in the 'front room,' where friends and neighbours could pay their last respects and mingle their tears with those of the bereaved family. Children, curious to see a dead body, were often taken to have 'one peep,' at the same time being encouraged to touch the corpse's hand to prevent their having nightmares.

It was a Derbyshire custom to place a sprig of thyme beside the body in the coffin. This was to keep away evil spirits and sometimes a dish of salt was left nearby for the same purpose.

The corpse was never left alone in case the devil stole it away and, as an added safeguard on the night before the burial, it was watched from dusk until dawn, members of the family taking turns in this custom known as 'lych-waking.'

Preparations for the funeral meal were made in advance and there have been many anecdotes of the dying person making an unexpected recovery and taking a share in it. There is a popular Derbyshire belief that dough will not rise in a house that contains a dead body, be it animal or human.

Every curtain and blind in the house remained closely drawn until after the funeral.

BURIAL

Unlike weddings, a funeral was an event for which no expense was spared. Sacrifices were made and often debts were incurred to ensure that the deceased had a 'proper send-off.' Many families put aside a few coppers each week, sometimes the mother and children being deprived of adequate meals as a result, so that a respectable funeral could be paid for.

PAUPER'S BURIAL

People who could not find the necessary fees were forced to make do with a 'pauper's burial,' all too common in the case of young childen's funerals for their death rate until the 20th century was grievously high.

Similarly, householders who, until the late 19th century, were held responsible for providing a 'decent burial' for anyone who died in their house, had to rely on 'the parish' if they were unable to find the means.

In most places there were funds from some charity, often established as far back as the 17th century when there was no poor law, which could supply the cost of a shroud if not a coffin. Many people were buried only in shrouds but, in some villages, there was a 'parish coffin,' kept in the parish church. This was used over and over again for the funerals of poor people.

At Ashover, the charge for a burial was '19 pence if ye corpse be coffined, 17 pence if wrapped in a shroude.'

On the day before the funeral two friends of the family would go round the village inviting one representative from each household to attend the ceremony. These guests who were 'bidden to the berrin' would go back to the house afterwards and partake of a substantial meal which included wine and 'berrin cake.'

It was not unusual for some favourite possessions belonging to the deceased, like a pipe or a mug or a family photograph, to be placed in the coffin together with his false teeth. This followed a primitive belief that such things might be required in the After Life. In the sheep rearing areas of Derbyshire it was customary to place in the coffin a piece of wool thus indicating to the Almighty that, because of his occupation, the deceased had been unable to attend church regularly.

The body, feet first, with or without a coffin, was carried out of the house either through a window or through the front door, never the back. The bearers, usually friends or relatives of the deceased and often his grandsons, were given a drink of 'funeral wine' before picking up the coffin.

There was a belief, still held in some parts of Derbyshire, that if, on the way to church, the corpse was caried over private land, its route should, in future, become a public right of way.

MOURNERS

It was important to have an even number of mourners who followed the hearse in pairs, those most closely related to the departed walking first, for, according to a Derbyshire superstition, anyone who walked alone at a funeral would be the next to be buried.

LYCHGATE, WINGERWORTH

photo — M. Burton

Members representing a club to which the deceased had belonged often walked by the side of the hearse.

Horses with nodding black plumes, black hatbands for the men and black veils for the ladies were essential accompaniments to the funeral ceremonial.

Arriving at the entrance to the churchyard, the bearers halted under the sloping roof of the lychgate and rested the coffin on the wooden shelf provided for the purpose. This pause was made to await the arrival of the clergyman who then led the cortège into church.

SIN EATERS

An old graveside practice took place when the corpse was about to be buried. First a piece of bread and then a bowl of beer was passed over the body and these were eaten and drunk by some poor person for an arranged payment, usually sixpence. In doing so it was believed that he was taking upon himself all the sins of the deceased who could thus be certain of a place in heaven.

BURYING UPSIDE DOWN

Any woman suspected of being a witch was buried upside down like the Poolsbrook woman, Mary Baines. She was buried that way so that, as the sexton said, she could not 'get out that road.'

The last person to be buried before a churchyard became full and was declared closed was also placed in the grave in this position. This was to prevent other corpses pushing him out.

Sometimes a dog was killed and buried in a churchyard newly opened because of the belief that the devil could claim the first corpse to go into newly consecrated ground.

THE DEVIL'S SIDE

The north side of a village churchyard was known as the 'Devil's Side' for this part which had not been consecrated by the bishop was reserved for the burial of unbaptised children, criminals and suicides.

STILLBORN infants and those who had died before being christened were usually interred at night without a funeral service. However, if a local adult was being buried at about that time, the child was placed in the same coffin or buried alongside. This procedure was welcomed by relatives of the dead person as it was believed that, in the company of a sinless child, the deceased would be readily admitted to the Life Everlasting.

In the 18th century many criminals were buried in Saint Peter's churchyard, Derby. These included Anne Williamson who was executed on August 1st 1755 for picking men's pockets at Ashbourne Fair.

SUICIDES could, with the permission of the clergyman, be laid to rest on the north side of a churchyard but without a funeral service. In April 1600 Isabelle Taylor, a widow who had drowned herself in a well, was buried in the graveyard at Chesterfield but it used to be the custom for suicides to be buried at a crossroads, after sunset, sometimes with a stake through their body.

In 1573 Thomas Maule who lived near Hardwick was found 'hunge on a tree by the wayside after a drunken fitte.' Following the coroner's inquest, held according to custom in the church porch, he was buried 'at midnighte at ye crossroads with a stake in him.' It was said that crowds of people from 'Mansfelde' were spectators at the event.

This method of dealing with suicides was abolished in 1823.

MAIDENS' GARLANDS, TRUSLEY
photo — C. E. Brown

MAIDENS' GARLANDS

A young woman who died soon after her wedding was traditionally buried in her bridal gown and an unmarried girl was dressed in white and carried to church by her friends. A girl of the same age walked before the coffin carrying a paper garland. After the service, this was hung in church over the pew of the dead girl's parents, together with a pair of white paper gloves, symbols of purity.

The only places in Derbyshire where these garlands or 'crantses' have been preserved are in St. Giles's church, Matlock, where five of them are on display in a glass case, at Trusley where a single one is similarly kept on view and at Ashford-in-the-Water where four of them are found hanging from the beams, the gloves suspended beside them.

FUNERAL DOLES

The distribution of gloves to the mourners at the funeral of an affluent person was an old custom in Derbyshire but the practice of providing dole money for poor people often led to disorder among the large crowd of vagrants who surrounded the church where the burial was to take place.

At the funeral of Bess of Hardwick's husband, the Earl of Shrewsbury, at Sheffield in 1591, about 20,000 poor persons turned up in the hope of receiving alms. Some years later, William Savile of Beeley directed in his will that the dole money on the day of the funeral should be given 'only to certain chosen, discreet, sober persons in the neighbouring parishes.'

FUNERAL TEA

After the interment, relatives and close friends returned to the house of the deceased for the enjoyment of the lavish spread of food and drink provided. There were always one or two who, having over-indulged, had to be trundled home in a wheelbarrow.

In the 18th century the Overseers of the Poor for the parish of All Saints in Derby supplied ale for the funeral of poor persons and St. Werburgh's, Derby, provided three-cornered burial buns at the funerals of children of the poor.

A book in my possession containing records of the Gisborne Charity Disbursement at Wingerworth includes details of payments made to James Norman who, in 1805, was receiving 5 shillings every two weeks for subsistence. After he died the charity paid 2 shillings for laying him out, 10 shillings and sixpence for his coffin, half a crown for the undertaker's fees and, FOR ALE AT THE FUNERAL 5 shillings, the same amount he had been allowed to live on for a fortnight.

BODY SNATCHING

By the beginning of the 19th century body-snatching had become a flourishing trade. Information having been received about a newly buried corpse, the 'Resurrection Cart' would make a silent journey, late at night, to the churchyard containing the new grave.

The bodies were stolen for the purpose of use in dissection by medical students and the practice was widely condoned by surgeons, sometimes encouraged by them to the extent of paying for a man to be murdered and used for anatomy study. Only the naked corpse was stolen for a much more severe penalty could be imposed for taking the burial clothes as well.

Midnight excursions by 'Resurrectionists' from Manchester and Sheffield frequently crossed the county border into Derbyshire and relatives of deceased persons sat night after night by the graves, armed with cudgels, until it was assumed that the bodies would no longer be of use for dissection.

Two examples of body-snatching are recorded in the Parish Registers at Hope.

1831 October 26th William Radwell aged 28. Body stolen during night following burial.

1834 October 2nd Benjamin Wrags of Bradwell, aged 21. Body stolen from grave.

MOURNING

All relations and friends who had been present at the funeral were expected to attend the church service on the following Sunday morning when 'mourning hymns' were sung and a funeral sermon was preached.

From that time the bereaved family were supposed to withdraw from social life for several months, the widow remaining in isolation for a year except to make regular visits to her husband's grave.

In the 19th century Mourning was Big Business and a graduated scale of dress was fixed according to the degree of relationship to the Departed.

'This, Madam,' explained an assistant in an old established Chesterfield firm, speaking in suitably lugubrious tones, 'is the

Light Affliction Department. The Heavy Bereavement is further on.'

Close relatives wore deepest black for a year. Widows enshrouded themselves in 'weeds' for the rest of their lives and few of them remarried although it was expected that a widower would seek another wife after a seemly interval had elapsed.

Black bordered funeral cards were sent out and writing paper, deeply edged in black, was used for all correspondence which invariably contained a reference to the writer's overwhelming sorrow.

Today, no outward signs either in dress or in behaviour indicate that someone has suffered a loss. Bereaved husbands, wives or mothers feel they are expected to stifle their emotions and guard against exhibiting their distress.

'The bellowing cow is the first to forget its calf,' is a Derbyshire saying and it is true that, by giving vent to one's feelings, tension is released and mental strain reduced. It is possible that the Victorians who exposed their grief so unashamedly recovered more quickly than the mourners of today who make such determined efforts to suppress it.

PREPARATIONS IN ADVANCE

Some Derbyshire people made arrangements for their burial well before they died.

According to her wishes, Florence Nightingale was carried to her grave by six veterans of the Crimean War and the modest inscription on her tombstone says nothing more than, 'F.N. Born 1820. Died 1910.'

The gravestone of Alison Uttley, Derbyshire author of the 'Little Grey Rabbit' books, bears only the words she had suggested, 'Alison Uttley, a Spinner of Tales.'

In contrast is the ornate tomb of Bess of Hardwick in Derby Cathedral, erected several years before her death. She ordered her effigy to be made in alabaster so that it 'wanted nothing but setting up' and she directed that her funeral be 'not too sumptuous.'

Leonard Wheatcroft, the 17th century Parish Clerk of Ashover, found an old stone coffin and gave instructions for it to be placed in a grave in the churchyard ready for his burial. The coffin was discovered in 1880. It contained several large bones and a piece of lead bearing the words, 'Here was Leonard Wheatcroft buried, aged 80. 1706.

Anthony Bradshaw of Farnah Hall, Duffield, had his tomb installed in Duffield church in 1600 and he lived for another 14 years. Engraved on the tomb are portraits of himself, his two wives and 20 children, complete with their initials. Before he died he had fathered three more children. In his will he left money for almshouses for the occupation of four old women

ANTHONY BRADSHAW'S TOMB, DUFFIELD   *photo — Derbys. Life & Countryside*

of Duffield with the proviso that they kept his tomb dusted. After the almshouses were pulled down in 1884, the land was sold and the proceeds invested to provide £1 every half year for four old ladies to continue dusting his tomb. This they do after morning service every Sunday and each is supplied with a feather duster.

MEMORIALS

'*Praises on tombs are trifles vainly spent.*
A man's good name is his best monument.'

In the early days of Christianity, burial of the dead in churches was prohibited. This led to churches being erected OVER the graves of martyrs. Later, interments within the precincts were allowed only for high dignitaries of the church or manorial lords. Cemeteries were established for the burial of ordinary people.

The burying of the dead in churchyards did not begin until the 8th century and headstones were erected only for important or wealthy people. Graves of the lower classes were identified by rough, wooden crosses set in mounds of earth over the corpse.

Epitaphs on tombs began to gain popularity in the 18th century. Many of these tended to be more lengthy than accurate and received much criticism, conveyed in one case by the following added to the original inscription.

'*Friend, in your epitaph I'm grieved,*
So very much is said,
One half will never be believed,
The other never read.'

There were time-honoured verses found in every country churchyard like the one at Castleton.

'*If all mankind would live in mutual love,*
This world would much resemble that above.'

Some were quite original, written by the people themselves

before they died. Inscribed on the tombstone of Ruth Coates, erected at Youlgreave in 1799, we read,

'Adieu, vain world, I've had enough of thee,
I'm now regardless of what thou sayest of me.'

In Bolsover churchyard is a tombstone carrying the date 1836 and the words,

'Here lies in a horizontal position the outside case of Thomas Hinde, Clock and Watchmaker, who departed this life wound up in the hope of being taken in hand by his Maker and being thoroughly cleaned, repaired and set a-going in the world to come.'

Leonard Wheatcroft of Ashover composed many epitaphs for friends who had passed away. On the death of his mother who had 'practised rare cures' he wrote,

'From us she's gone. I hope her soul's ascended
To live with Christ for thousands she has mended.'

Beneath the ancient yew tree in Allestree churchyard is the grave of Edmund Buxton and his wife, Joanna. Edmund died in 1790, aged 32, and his inscription addresses his wife.

To this must thou come, Remember and be ready.'

It was 47 years before Joanna was buried beside him and

ALLESTREE CHURCHYARD

her reply reads,

'My love, I am come and have endeavoured to be ready.'

Stained glass windows, brasses, effigies and commemorative wall tablets abound in Derbyshire churches. The most beautiful and poignant of these must surely be the marble

TOMB OF PENELOPE BOOTHBY, ASHBOURNE CHURCH
photo — Derbyshire Life and Countryside

figure in St. Oswald's church, Ashbourne, of Penelope Boothby who died, aged 5 years, in 1791. The only child of Sir Brooke and Dame Susannah Boothby, her epitaph reads,

'She was in form and intellect most exquisite. The unfortunate parents ventured their all on this frail Bark and the wreck was total.'

SOURCES

Ancient Customs of Derbyshire	Crichton Porteous
Old English Customs	Roy Christian
Derbyshire	Roy Christian
The Illustrated History of Derbyshire	John Heath
Old Wives' Tales	Mary Chamberlain
Derbyshire Folklore	John Merrill
Folklore and Customs of Rural England	Margaret Baker
Citizen's Derby	Alfred Richardson
History of Chesterfield	J. M. Bestall
Hanged for a Sheep	E. G. Power
West End Story	Elsie Elizabeth Goodhead
May the Lord have mercy on your soul	Philip Taylor
Domestic Life in England	Nora Lofts
And the Bride Wore . . .	Ann Monsarrat
Country Voices	Charles Kightly
Derbyshire Notes and Queries	Thompson
The Derbyshire Guide	Derbyshire Life and Countryside
Derbyshire Characters for Young People	Elizabeth Eisenberg
Dorothy	Joy Childs
The Healer's Art	John Camp

Author's note:
Although I have supplied a list of books used in compiling 'from the Cradle to the Grave,' I have to say that most of its contents are drawn from the memories of my upbringing and early life in a north Derbyshire village.